Andrea Minoglio   Laura Fanelli

Our World OUT OF BALANCE

Understanding Climate Change
— • — *and* — • —
What We Can Do

CONTENTS

WHEN THE WORLD GETS WARMER

Not too cold, not too hot. That's how Earth's temperature has always been. At an average of 58°F (14.4°C), it's been perfect for supporting life. Most other known planets are not so lucky. Mercury's average temperature, for instance, is 338°F (170°C). That's as hot as an oven! We're lucky because the sun's rays are filtered by our **atmosphere** and its gases. Our atmosphere is like a blanket protecting us from the cold of outer space. But since the Industrial Revolution, the average temperature has gone up by about 1.8°F (1°C). Since 1998, it has been getting higher every year. This rising temperature is called **global warming**. Our blanket has now begun to keep us a bit too warm.

Global warming is one part of **climate change**. Climate change means increasing changes in many climate patterns over a long period of time. For example, more or less rain, hotter or colder temperatures, or stronger wind. It's like Earth has a fever. Having a fever isn't good—you must try to bring it down. The overwhelming majority of scientists agree that humans' own actions are the reason for our warming climate.

BEFORE For nearly 800,000 years, until 1950, the average amount of **carbon dioxide** (CO_2) in the atmosphere always stayed below 300 parts per million. (That's a measurement for how much of a substance is present.)

Earth's average temperature has gone up and down many times throughout history because of natural causes.

WHY STOP GLOBAL WARMING?

As it gets warmer, Earth's seasons will change. Without frost, plants will flower for longer before they make seeds. This could be a big problem for farmers growing crops.

Many animals, in the sea and on land, may have to find new homes. Some may even become **extinct** (see p. 24).

When temperatures rise, so does the risk of fires (see p. 56). Fires can do great damage and release a lot of carbon dioxide into the atmosphere.

As our world heats up, some insects that are harmful to humans and crops may move into places that were too cold for them before.

... AND AFTER Between 1950 and 2020, the amount of carbon dioxide in the air has risen to about 412 parts per million!

Since 2001, we have had nineteen of the hottest years ever.

By 2100, scientists predict it could be 3.6°F (2°C) hotter than it was in 1880. Their worst-case prediction is the temperature could go up by more than 9°F (5°C)!

5

HOW THE GREENHOUSE EFFECT WORKS

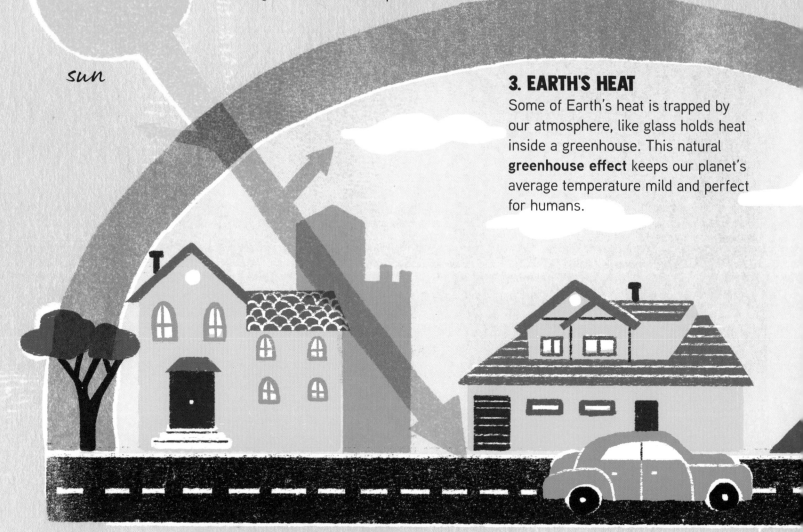

1. THE ATMOSPHERE
Our planet is wrapped in a layer of air. This is a mixture of gases called the atmosphere. The atmosphere filters the sun's rays, letting some rays pass through to Earth and bouncing the rest back into space.

2. THE SUN'S RAYS ARE ABSORBED
Some of the sun's rays are reflected by ice, snow, water, grass, and sand. And some rays are absorbed by Earth's seas and land, warming them up.

3. EARTH'S HEAT
Some of Earth's heat is trapped by our atmosphere, like glass holds heat inside a greenhouse. This natural **greenhouse effect** keeps our planet's average temperature mild and perfect for humans.

sun

HOW YOU CAN HELP

There are many things you can do to help combat global warming each and every day. For example, you can choose to eat only local, seasonal foods. Those foods are grown close by and don't use fuel to travel far. You can find out about your food by checking the labels in the supermarket, or you can buy food directly from growers at your local farmers' market.

Or you can write to your mayor, governor, and state and federal legislators to ask them to support strong, smart environmental policy. A postcard writing party can be fun with family or friends!

If you do these small acts regularly, they will add up over time. Get others to join you, and you can—and will!—make big changes.

4. TOO MANY GREENHOUSE GASES

We are releasing a lot of extra **greenhouse gases** into our atmosphere, beyond what is normal. **Pollution** does this; it is mostly caused by humans using **fossil fuels** (coal, oil, and gasoline). The additional greenhouse gases trap too much heat. This causes the planet to get hotter.

heat

THE HOLE IN THE OZONE LAYER

Earth's atmosphere contains a layer of **ozone**. This filters the sun's ultraviolet rays that can cause skin cancer and other diseases. In the 1980s, scientists noticed that this "sunscreen" protecting Earth was getting very thin in spots. In 1987, many countries agreed to ban the use of some gases (mostly those used in refrigerators and aerosols) that were causing this hole in the ozone layer. Look what happened! Between 2000 and 2017, the hole got smaller. In fact, the hole in 2017 was the smallest it had been since 1988. The ozone layer continues to be on the road to recovery!

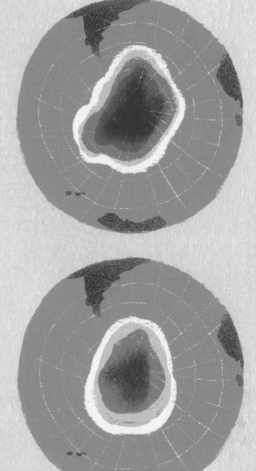

The hole in the ozone layer in 2000 was 11.4 million square miles.

The hole in the ozone layer in 2017 was 7.2 million square miles.

HOW PEOPLE ARE HELPING

In the early 1990s, countries started signing on to support the United Nations Framework Convention on Climate Change. Since 1995, these countries have met every year for a Conference of the Parties (COP) to talk about what they're doing to fight climate change. At COP21, the twenty-first conference, 195 countries from all around the world met in Paris. There, many signed the Paris Agreement to stop Earth's temperature from rising by more than 3.6°F (2°C) above the 1880 temperature. They agreed to try to keep the increase below 2.7°F (1.5°C). That goal will take some doing. To reach that target, all the world's **emissions** must be cut in half by 2030. We can do it if everyone works together. COP26 is scheduled to happen in 2021 in Glasgow, Scotland.

RISING SEA LEVELS

Do you love jumping into the ocean? Or snorkeling and looking for fish? Or playing in the surf with friends? But it's not so great if the ocean comes right into town, maybe even flooding your home. Sadly, there's a risk this may soon happen to millions of people living on the coasts all over the world. Because of global warming (see p. 4), the sea's level has risen nearly ten inches over the last 150 years. We need to do something fast if we don't want to be swamped by water.

BEFORE

Seas and oceans cover 71 percent of Earth's surface. They're very important and useful to us all, in so many different ways.

600 million humans live in low-lying areas (three to sixty-five feet above sea level), which are more likely to flood.

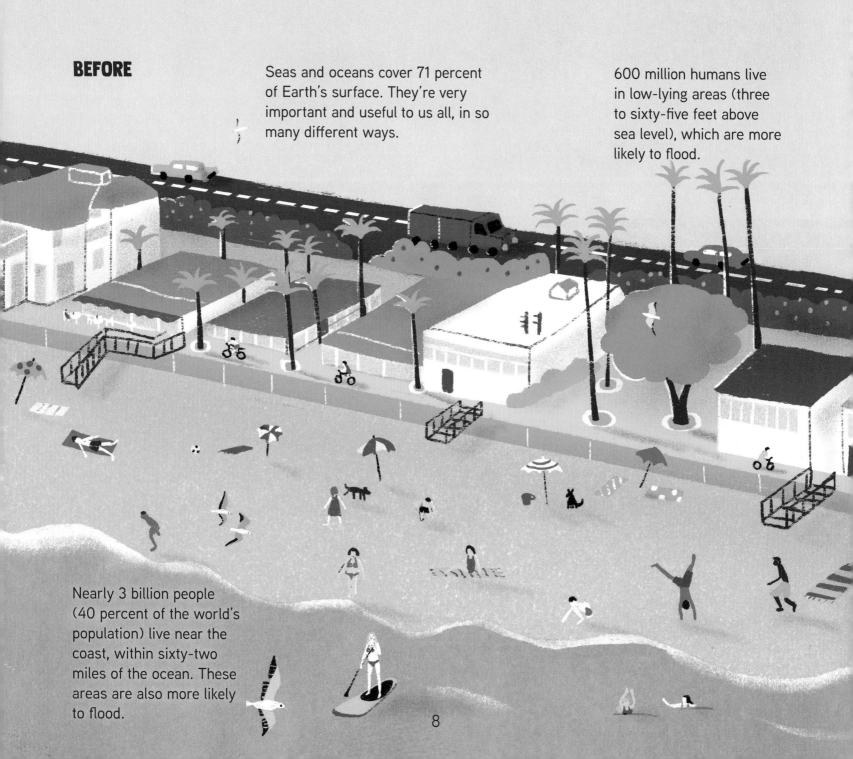

Nearly 3 billion people (40 percent of the world's population) live near the coast, within sixty-two miles of the ocean. These areas are also more likely to flood.

WHY STOP SEA LEVELS FROM RISING?

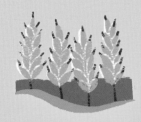

When seawater spreads inland, it hurts crops and contaminates drinking water.

Flooding would leave millions of people who live near the sea without homes or food. They would have to find new places to live. This would increase the population in other countries.

Some islands in the Pacific Ocean, like Kiribati, stand just a few feet above sea level. Soon, these could be covered completely by rising seas. Even some big cities are already "sinking" in the rising waters. These include Venice, Italy; Rotterdam, Netherlands; Miami, USA; Bangkok, Thailand; and Jakarta, Indonesia. Soon, they'll be in serious trouble too.

... AND AFTER

Scientists have calculated that every time the sea level rises 0.4 inches, 6 million people are at risk from flooding.

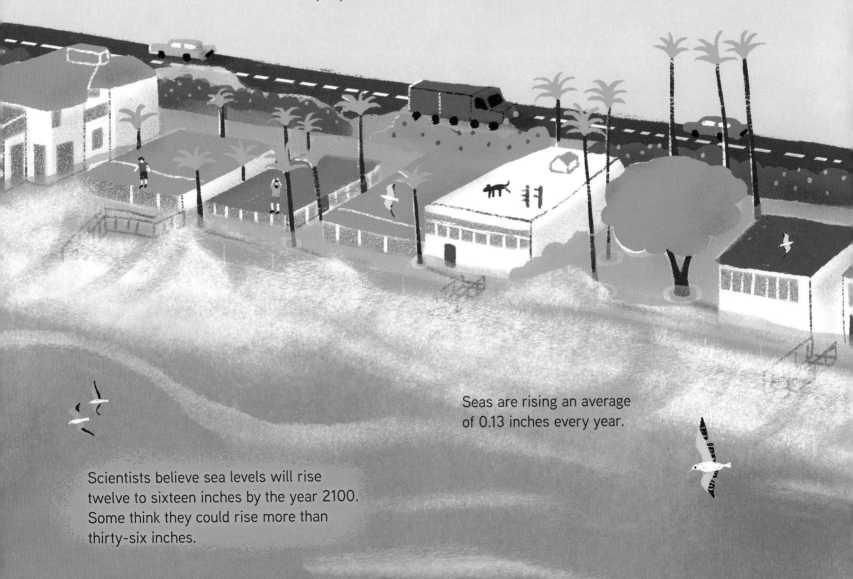

Seas are rising an average of 0.13 inches every year.

Scientists believe sea levels will rise twelve to sixteen inches by the year 2100. Some think they could rise more than thirty-six inches.

HOW AND WHY SEA LEVELS RISE

1. THE "NORMAL" LEVEL

If you put a balloon full of air next to a flame, the heat will burst it right away. But a balloon full of water takes much longer to pop. That's because water heats up more slowly than air and absorbs 1,000 times more heat. On Earth, our oceans absorb most of the heat produced by global warming (93 percent).

2. THE LEVEL RISES BECAUSE IT'S HOTTER

But oceans have begun to heat up too. And they swell as they get hotter. This expansion is causing a third of the rise in sea levels. So the same amount of water in Earth's oceans takes up more space because it is hotter.

HOW YOU CAN HELP

Beaches and sand dunes form a natural barrier against rising oceans. Walk on beach paths so you don't damage the dunes. Wetlands along the coast (like lagoons and salt marshes) also help to stop flooding. Some studies show they might also protect against global warming because they absorb a lot of carbon dioxide. Pick up any trash you find there, even if it's not yours.

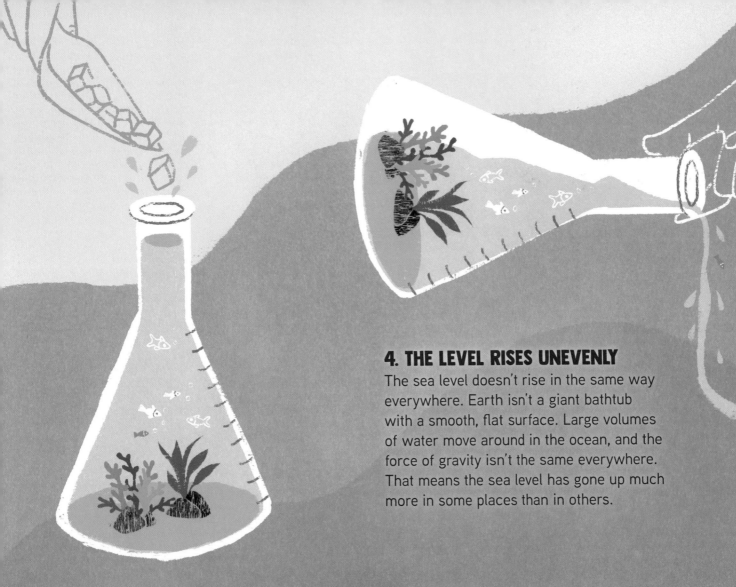

4. THE LEVEL RISES UNEVENLY

The sea level doesn't rise in the same way everywhere. Earth isn't a giant bathtub with a smooth, flat surface. Large volumes of water move around in the ocean, and the force of gravity isn't the same everywhere. That means the sea level has gone up much more in some places than in others.

3. THE ICE SHEETS ARE MELTING

The other two-thirds of the sea level rise is caused by melting continental ice sheets. These huge areas of ice covering dry land are mainly in Antarctica and Greenland. As the ice melts, more water pours into the sea. This causes levels to rise even higher.

These living sea walls are better at decreasing wave energy. Plus, they get bigger and more stable over time, as sediment is trapped and plants grow.

In Alabama, the Nature Conservancy is adding square wire cages to their sea walls. In time, marsh plants will grow inside the cages. They will turn the hard structures into a living shoreline that will help decrease wave power and flooding.

HOW PEOPLE ARE HELPING

Some people think building sea walls is the only way to keep rising seas out of cities and coastal communities. But sea walls and other hard structures cause lots of problems. They deflect wave energy and cause damage to other areas, and they often harm animals and **habitats** around them.

Fortunately, scientists are devising better methods. They are creating **living shorelines**, which usually means restoring what used to be there. It could mean creating a salt marsh or planting a mangrove forest.

SHRINKING FORESTS

Did you know that plants breathe? That's why people call large forests "Earth's lungs." Plants make their own food through **photosynthesis**, a process that uses sunlight, carbon dioxide, and water. During photosynthesis, plants absorb carbon dioxide and then release oxygen back into the air. In fact, more than half of Earth's oxygen is produced by algae and tiny plants called phytoplankton that live on the ocean's surface. So the problem with shrinking forests is not that we won't have enough oxygen. There is a different, real problem with **deforestation**. (This means cutting down a large number of trees or even entire forests in order to use the land for other purposes). The problem is the releasing of too much carbon dioxide. When plants are destroyed, not only do they stop absorbing carbon dioxide—they also release all the carbon dioxide stored inside them. This adds to the greenhouse effect and makes our planet hotter (see p. 4).

BEFORE

About 31 percent of Earth's land is covered with forests.

There are 750 million people, including 60 million indigenous people, living in forests.

WHY SAVE THE FORESTS?

 Forests are home to a huge variety of animals and plants. Around 80 percent of animal species live in forests. Some of those animals are in danger of going extinct because of deforestation (see p. 24).

 Living forests continue to grow and absorb carbon dioxide. If they die or get sick, they begin to give off carbon dioxide, releasing more than they take in.

 Without trees, the ground gradually wears away, making landslides more likely.

 Forests play an important part in the water cycle. Where there are fewer trees, there is less rainfall, and the land becomes drier.

... AND AFTER

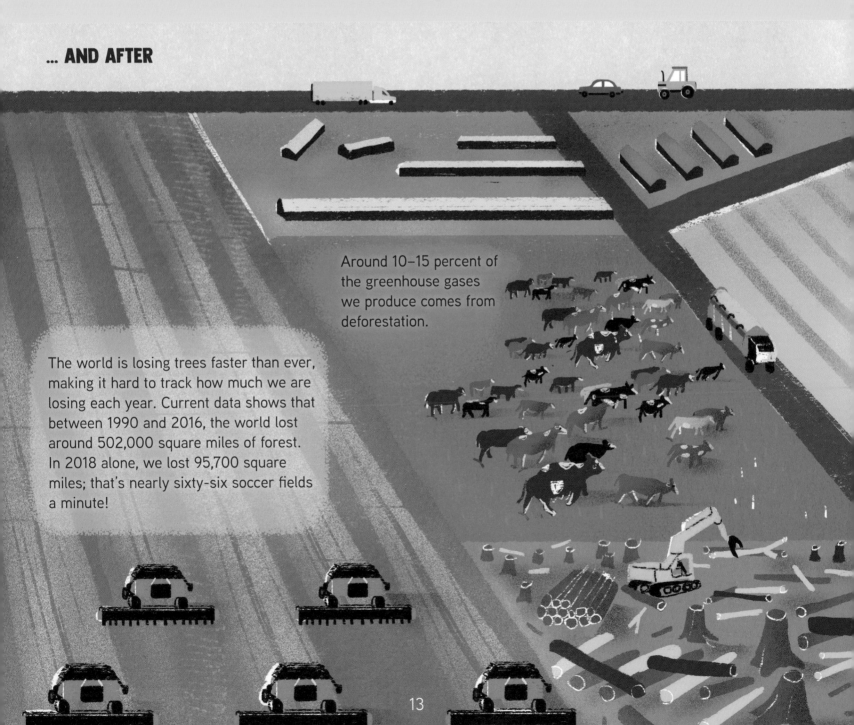

Around 10–15 percent of the greenhouse gases we produce comes from deforestation.

The world is losing trees faster than ever, making it hard to track how much we are losing each year. Current data shows that between 1990 and 2016, the world lost around 502,000 square miles of forest. In 2018 alone, we lost 95,700 square miles; that's nearly sixty-six soccer fields a minute!

HOW THE AMAZON RAINFOREST WORKS

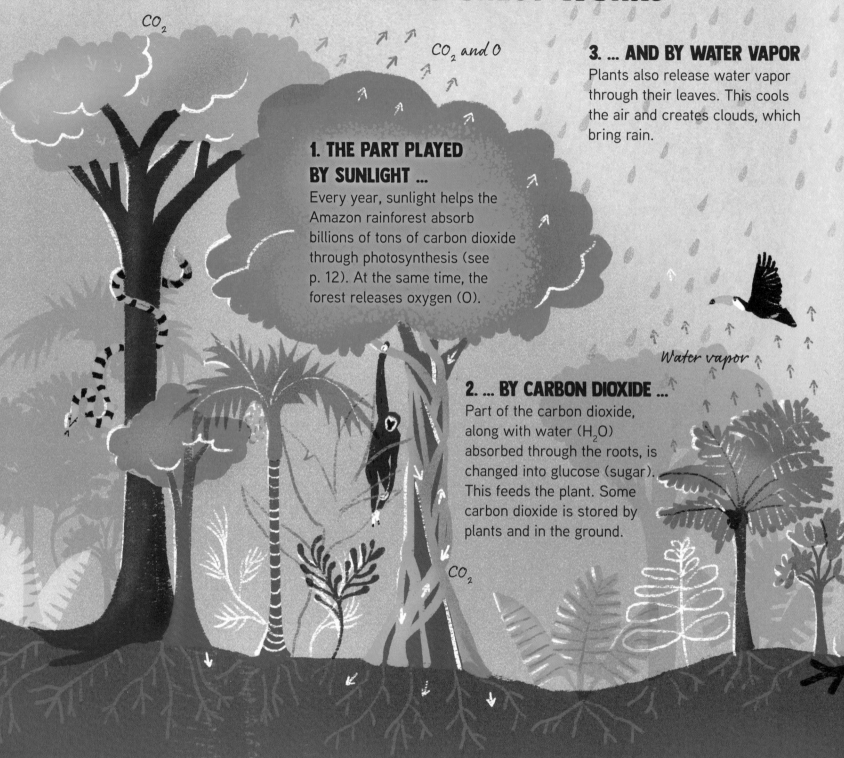

CO_2

CO_2 and O

3. ... AND BY WATER VAPOR
Plants also release water vapor through their leaves. This cools the air and creates clouds, which bring rain.

1. THE PART PLAYED BY SUNLIGHT ...
Every year, sunlight helps the Amazon rainforest absorb billions of tons of carbon dioxide through photosynthesis (see p. 12). At the same time, the forest releases oxygen (O).

2. ... BY CARBON DIOXIDE ...
Part of the carbon dioxide, along with water (H_2O) absorbed through the roots, is changed into glucose (sugar). This feeds the plant. Some carbon dioxide is stored by plants and in the ground.

Water vapor

CO_2

HOW YOU CAN HELP

Plant something! Trees are very important for our planet's climate, but all plants are important. Other plants, like flowers and vegetables, also take in carbon dioxide and release oxygen. You can become a **guerrilla gardener** by planting flowers or vegetables in empty public spaces (like empty lots or at your school). Also, paper is made from trees, so don't waste it! Use both sides of the paper when you're writing or drawing.

14

4. THE RELEASE OF CARBON DIOXIDE

If trees are cut down or burned, the stored carbon dioxide is released back into the atmosphere. This increases the temperature.

CO_2

5. DEATH OF THE FOREST

When it gets hotter and the air gets drier, plants cool down by sucking more water out of the ground. But less rain means less water in the ground. As the forest struggles to survive with less water, plants will release more carbon dioxide.

WHY DOES THIS HAPPEN?

Farming is the biggest cause of deforestation. The more people there are in the world, the more food we need. The more food we need, the more farmland we need. To make space for more crops or animal grazing, people are cutting down large numbers of trees. People also cut down trees for wood to make everything from your bedroom furniture to the pencil and paper you write with. Removing trees makes room for towns and roads. Fires are another big problem (see p. 56) for trees. As it gets hotter (p. 4), fires spread more easily, are harder to control, and destroy more trees.

HOW PEOPLE ARE HELPING

Kids Saving the Rainforest is an organization that Janine Licare and Aislin Livingstone started in Costa Rica in 1999, when they were just nine years old. The girls sold papier-mâché bottles and painted rocks, and they used their earnings to buy trees. They planted thousands of trees in the nearby forest. They also set up other projects to help save wildlife that live in the forests.

MORE CITIES, BIGGER CITIES

Even though cities take up just 3 percent of Earth's land surface, they are home to more than half the world's population (4.2 billion people). That's a huge number of people living in a very small space. In the future, there will be even more of us. By 2050, 2.5 billion *more* people will likely be living in cities, especially in Asia and Africa. That means more concrete, more roads, more buildings, more air pollution, more energy used, and more garbage. It also means more megalopolises, cities with over 10 million people. Right now, there are thirty-three megalopolises in the world. In ten years, there will be forty-three. But urbanization could actually be good news for the planet. Urbanization means building new cities or making them bigger. If we build cities vertically (more tall buildings), we use less land. Some scientists think cities will do less damage than if the growing population lives outside cities, spread out over a larger area.

BEFORE

In 1950, just 30 percent of the world's population lived in cities.

Many people think the first city was Eridu, built around 6,500 years ago in Mesopotamia.

WHY MANAGE THE GROWTH OF CITIES?

Heat waves happen more often and are more dangerous in cities. When it's hotter than usual for at least five days, that's a heat wave. Cities are **heat islands**, which means they get extra hot.

Big cities also produce loads of garbage. Garbage can pollute the environment and the water supply if not disposed of safely.

If a city is spread out over a huge area, then the land where animals and plants live is broken up by roads, railways, and buildings. That makes it hard for plants and animals to survive and puts some species in danger.

... AND AFTER

Today, more than 55 percent of the world's population lives in cities. By 2050, it will be 68 percent.

WHAT IS AN URBAN HEAT ISLAND, AND HOW DOES IT WORK?

1. OUTSIDE THE ISLAND

Maybe you've noticed it. When you ride your bike through a park on a hot day, you feel a little cooler, like the temperature dropped a few degrees. That's because you've just come out of the urban heat island. This is a part of the city that's hotter than its surroundings (the countryside, suburbs, or big parks). Why is that?

2. HOW PLANTS HELP

Plants give us shade, but they also absorb water through their roots and release it as water vapor through little holes underneath their leaves. This is called **transpiration**, and it helps keep the air cool, like nature's air conditioner. That's why it's hotter in parts of the city where fewer plants grow.

HOW YOU CAN HELP

Air-conditioning cools the inside of buildings and cars. It also pushes a lot of hot air outside, and it uses up energy. Turn it on as little as possible. If you do use it, keep your doors and windows closed, so it works without waste. To keep your house cool without AC, lower your blinds, close your curtains, and use a fan. Plant a tree! There are many organizations working to plant trees in cities across the world. Perhaps you can find one to volunteer with and plant some trees in your own neighborhood!

3. HEAT FROM ROADS

The sun's rays don't easily reflect off roads, concrete buildings, or any dark-colored surfaces. Instead, the light is absorbed and turned into heat, which is released at night. Also, waterproof road surfaces don't absorb rain. That means less water evaporates from the ground, which would cool the air in the same way that plants do.

5. HEAT BUILDS UP

An urban heat island is between 1°F (0.56°C) and 10°F (5.6°C) hotter than surrounding areas. You can feel the difference more at night or if the city has a lot of plants or trees around it. In the future, scientists think average temperatures in some cities could increase by 14°F (7.8°C) and get as hot as 122°F (50°C)!

4. HEAT FROM MOTORS

Heat is also produced by factories, cars, and anything that uses a motor. The hotter it gets, the more air-conditioning we use in our homes, cars, and offices. But that just makes it even hotter, so even more cooling is needed. It's a never-ending loop, like a cat chasing its own tail!

HOW PEOPLE ARE HELPING

To cool down heat islands, some cities are planting more green areas. Melbourne, Australia, plans to plant 3,000 new trees every year until 2040. In many cities, people are growing trees and plants on the tops of buildings. This creates **green roofs**. And in Los Angeles, California, some streets have been painted with a special white coating that reflects the sun's rays much better than the original, darker surface.

MELTING ICE

The parts of our planet that are covered with ice and snow are called the **cryosphere**. They include beautiful mountain glaciers and **permafrost**, areas that always remain frozen. They also include the **polar ice caps**, which are enormous masses of ice covering huge areas of the Antarctic and Greenland. Sea ice is the frozen surface of the ocean in the polar regions. Polar ice is six to ten feet thick, but in the summer, it melts a bit. This is to be expected. The problem is that for decades, all the snow and ice that make up Earth's cryosphere have been melting much more quickly than usual, and the cryosphere is getting smaller and smaller.

BEFORE

Around 10 percent of Earth's land and 12 percent of the seas are covered with ice. This ice reflects the light of the sun. That limits how much heat is absorbed and how much it warms up the land and oceans.

About 4 million people live in Arctic regions and 670 million in high mountains. In these areas, the beautiful ice and snow also attract tourists. They spend money that supports the people who live there.

WHY SAVE THE ICE?

Ice reflects the sun's rays, shielding us from global warming (see p. 4).

If the ice on land melts and flows into the sea, the sea level rises. Ice floating on water doesn't raise sea levels as it melts, but it can affect ocean currents and change the climate.

Seals live around the edges of sea ice. Polar bears eat seals. If there's no sea ice, polar bears have to travel very far to hunt. Often there is not enough to eat. Their survival is at risk.

In some parts of the planet, large amounts of gas are trapped in permafrost. When the permafrost melts, those gases will be released into the atmosphere. This could speed up global warming (see p. 4).

... AND AFTER

In recent years, Arctic sea ice has reduced by 13 percent every ten years. Summer sea ice is now half the size it was in 1980.

By 2050, if sea ice continues to melt, the number of polar bears will drop by two-thirds. Fewer than 10,000 polar bears will be left.

HOW POLAR SEA ICE IS FORMED

1. GREASE ICE

At the coldest time of the year, the surface of the sea begins to freeze over in some parts of the planet. Regular water freezes at 32°F (0°C), but seawater has to drop to 28.8°F (-1.8°C) to freeze because of the salt it contains. At the start of the freezing process, tiny crystals form. They grow until they become an oily-looking slush called grease ice.

2. PANCAKE ICE

The crystals grow until they join together into plates that are about three feet in diameter, called pancake ice.

3. NILAS

The pancake ice joins together until it forms a single sheet of ice about four inches thick. This slab of ice is called nilas. It bends with the waves below it but does not break.

HOW YOU CAN HELP

As ice in the Arctic melts, many energy companies want to drill for oil that lies deep beneath it. More oil means more global warming, which would make the problem of melting ice even worse. Instead of driving a car and using gas, walk or bike where you need to go, especially short distances. Ask your parents to leave the car at home and take the bus or train instead. When it's cold, don't waste energy! Put on a sweater instead of turning up the heat. If you're interested in polar bears, find out about environmental groups that are working to keep them safe.

4. YOUNG ICE

When the ice gets thicker than four inches, a hard layer forms that no longer bends with the waves. This is called young ice.

5. SUMMER MELT

When spring arrives and the weather gets warmer, the ice begins to melt. Arctic ice is thinnest at the end of summer.

6. OLD ICE

If the ice survives for one or more summers without melting, it is called old ice. But because of higher temperatures and global warming (see p. 4), not much old ice survives the heat, and the amount of new ice is getting smaller and smaller each year. Scientists believe that by 2050, sea ice will disappear completely in the summer.

HOW PEOPLE ARE HELPING

Leslie Field, an engineer at Stanford University, started a group called Ice911. They propose covering areas of Arctic ice with billions of tiny glass balls, called microspheres. These glass balls would reflect the sun's light and protect the ice, stopping it from melting so fast. These microspheres stick to the ice, but they don't pollute, and they aren't harmful to animals. Ice911's first experiments on a lake in Alaska were successful—the ice got thicker!

WHAT IS HAPPENING TO OUR WILDLIFE?

Maybe you've heard of the dodo. It was a bird that lived on the island of Mauritius and couldn't fly. In the 1500s, Portuguese sailors landed there. The humans cut down forests and brought in foreign animals like pigs, dogs, cats, and monkeys. They destroyed the dodo's natural habitat (the place where it can most easily survive). So the dodos went extinct. This is just one example of extinction, but it shows what is happening today too, on a larger scale, all over the world. Some scientists believe that a mass extinction, like what happened to the dinosaurs 65 million years ago, is happening now. A mass extinction is a huge drop in the number of species over a fairly short period of time. Some experts believe that 50 percent of Earth's species could go extinct before the end of this century. But this time we can't blame asteroids or gigantic volcanic explosions. This time it's our fault!

BEFORE

Biodiversity is the variety and quantity of living organisms (animals and plants) that live in a place.

Scientists believe there are 8.7 million species on Earth—6.5 million on land and 2.2 million in the oceans. They also believe that 90 percent of Earth's species haven't been discovered yet.

WHY PROTECT BIODIVERSITY?

Life on Earth, including human life, depends on the presence of many different species of plants, animals, and microorganisms. Many of our foods would be lost without pollinators (bees, wasps, butterflies, birds, and bats) to help plants form seeds.

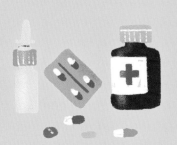

Many of our medicines come from plants and animals. Some lifesaving medicines could disappear before we even discover them.

Environments with lots of different plants and animals are rich in biodiversity. They are stronger and better able to cope with problems like climate change.

... AND AFTER

Scientists are tracking about 120,000 species. Of those, 32,000 could go extinct soon. That includes 26 percent of all mammals, 41 percent of amphibians, 14 percent of birds, and 30 percent of sharks and rays.

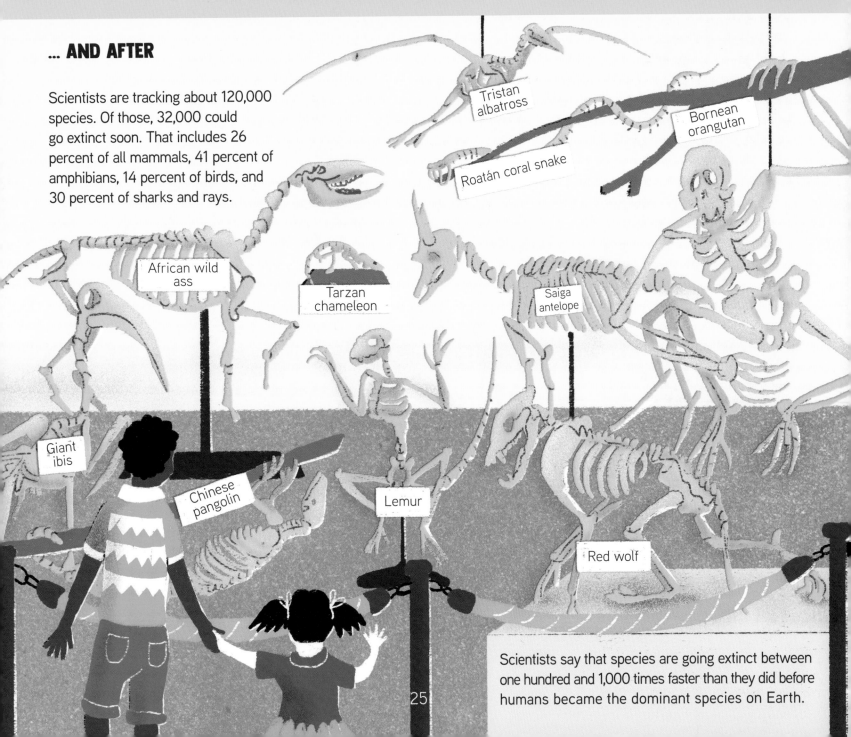

Tristan albatross

Bornean orangutan

Roatán coral snake

African wild ass

Tarzan chameleon

Saiga antelope

Giant ibis

Chinese pangolin

Lemur

Red wolf

Scientists say that species are going extinct between one hundred and 1,000 times faster than they did before humans became the dominant species on Earth.

HOW A SMALL BIRD BECOMES EXTINCT

1. A QUIET LIFE

The 'akikiki, a type of honeycreeper, is a small bird that used to pass its time peacefully chirping on the Hawaiian island of Kaua'i.

3. ESCAPE

To escape disease, the 'akikiki moved higher up into the mountains, where it was too cold for mosquitoes. Those birds survived, while most birds that lived lower on the island did not.

2. AN UNWELCOME VISITOR

When humans arrived on the island, they brought mosquito larvae, which had not existed there before. When the humans collected fresh water, the mosquito larvae fell into it. Humans also brought caged birds with them. Some of these had diseases. The new mosquitoes bit the sick birds and the healthy birds. Then all the birds carried the new diseases.

HOW YOU CAN HELP

One of the best ways to care about biodiversity is to learn more about it. Which plants and animals live in your area? How many are there? Grab a pen, a notebook, and a camera and go exploring! Follow your usual route but look up at the sky or down at the ground. You'll be surprised by how many birds and insects there are. See if you can recognize them. If you can't, look them up in a guidebook or ask someone who knows more. Then write a note in your logbook. Even if you don't see animals, you might see signs of them: feathers, hair, footprints, and ... poop! Share what you've discovered with your friends and family. Tell them why biodiversity is important. You can even join a **citizen science** project where you do research and share your data to help maintain biodiversity in your area.

5. EXTINCTION

If nothing changes, scientists say these birds will be extinct in ten to thirty years. That's what happened to a rodent (*Melomys rubicola*) that lived on the island of Bramble Cay, between Australia and New Guinea. In 2019, it was the first mammal to go extinct because of climate change.

4. DEATH

In recent years, as it has gotten warmer on Kaua'i, mosquitoes have begun moving up into the mountains. The birds can't go any higher, so they have started dying again. In the last fifteen years, the 'akikiki population has dropped by 98 percent.

WHY DOES THIS HAPPEN?

Some scientists think that our geological era, the Holocene era, should be renamed the **Anthropocene** era. That means "the new human era," because we humans have had such an impact on the planet and its climate. Not only are we causing global temperatures to rise, but we are destroying natural habitats, leading to the extinction of many animals and plants.

HOW PEOPLE ARE HELPING

All over the world, countries are creating nature reserves to protect animals and plants. Around 15 percent of Earth's land and 7 percent of the seas are now protected zones. But many scientists say that is not enough. They think at least 30 percent of the planet should be protected by 2030. This is one of the goals of the Convention on Biological Diversity, an agreement nearly 200 countries have signed. The agreement seeks to stop plants and animals from dying out. Also, the Earth BioGenome Project was launched in 2018. This project plans to identify the DNA of millions of species and make the information available to everyone. This work could help us better understand how to protect our endangered species.

EXTREME WEATHER EVENTS

Extreme weather events include scorching heat and drought (see p. 36) as well as rainstorms, hailstorms, floods, fires, tornadoes, and tropical cyclones. Tropical cyclones are massive storms with very strong winds. They form above the ocean, but they can reach land and may last for weeks. The longest cyclone on record lasted thirty-one days, in 1994. Tropical cyclones might have innocent-sounding names like Sandy, Katrina, Gilbert, and Mitch, but they can do terrible damage. But what does climate change have to do with these events? Scientists are still working on it, but they are fairly sure that some extreme weather events have gotten more violent because of climate change. It's hotter now, so more water vapor is being released into the atmosphere. Water vapor causes rain, and more of it causes heavier rainfall and hurricanes. If things don't change, there may not be more days of rain or more hurricanes, but they will almost surely be more severe. In other words, where it rains, it will rain much harder. And where it doesn't rain, it will become much drier.

BEFORE

Tropical cyclones have different names depending on where they begin. If they form over the Atlantic Ocean, they're called hurricanes. If they form above the Pacific Ocean, they're called typhoons.

In most places, about half the yearly rain and snow falls during just twelve days.

WHY STUDY EXTREME WEATHER EVENTS?

Every year, many people die or are left homeless because of heat waves, droughts, floods, and tropical cyclones.

Extreme weather events also do serious damage to business. Today, many businesses are international, which means countries around the world depend on each other. So, when an extreme weather event stops production of items in one part of the world, the financial losses impact people all over the world.

... AND AFTER

For every couple of degrees the temperature rises, water vapor in our atmosphere increases by 7 percent. This adds to the greenhouse effect (see p. 4) and causes heavier rain.

Between 1970 and 2012, there were 8,835 extreme weather events linked to climate change. These caused the deaths of nearly 2 million people.

HOW A TROPICAL CYCLONE STARTS

1. WARM WATER EVAPORATES

In the tropical band close to the equator, cyclones form above oceans. They form when the water temperature reaches at least 79°F (26°C). The warm water evaporates. This makes the air moist. The wind carries this wet air upward, where it cools down.

3. THE EYE OF THE CYCLONE

As the moist air keeps rising, winds begin to blow in a circle. The wind collects more and more clouds around a central point. This is called the eye of the cyclone. South of the equator, cyclones turn clockwise. North of the equator, they turn counterclockwise.

2. BIG CLOUDS FORM

The moist air condenses into little drops of water. These form into big clouds.

HOW YOU CAN HELP

To better understand extreme weather where you live, you can learn more about your day-to-day climate. Start a weather journal and keep track the daily temperature, rainfall, etc. In time, you will be able to answer questions like "Did it rain more this year than last year? How many days were hotter than average?" You can also help scientists learn more about extreme weather events and climate change. Share your weather information with them. Scientists rely on this kind of data from volunteers to understand how climate change is impacting areas around the world. You can share precipitation measurements with the Community Collaborative Rain, Hail and Snow Network. You can share drought information with the International Drought Experiment. Even NASA wants your data! Share your photos of clouds and sky conditions with the NASA GLOBE Observer program.

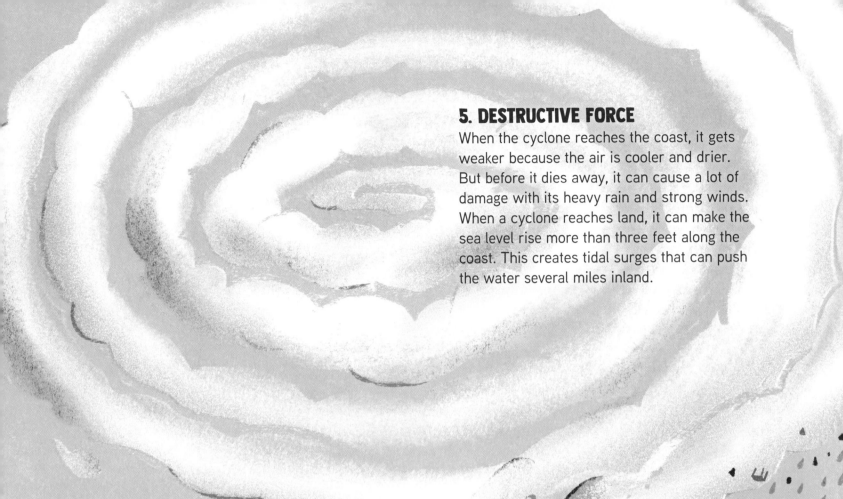

5. DESTRUCTIVE FORCE

When the cyclone reaches the coast, it gets weaker because the air is cooler and drier. But before it dies away, it can cause a lot of damage with its heavy rain and strong winds. When a cyclone reaches land, it can make the sea level rise more than three feet along the coast. This creates tidal surges that can push the water several miles inland.

4. HERE IT COMES ...

The spiraling clouds get bigger and bigger. When the winds turning them reach a speed of at least seventy-four miles per hour, they're called cyclones. Cyclones can be up to ten miles tall and 1,200 miles wide. The strongest ones are called category 5 cyclones. They reach speeds of over 138 miles per hour!

HOW PEOPLE ARE HELPING

Some think it might be possible to change the climate artificially, though not everyone agrees on how. One idea is to spray salt inside clouds to make them whiter. Then they would reflect more light. This could make the oceans colder and maybe stop cyclones from forming. Other researchers have suggested cooling the seas by using a floating pump to pull up deeper, colder water and mixing it with warmer surface water. Of course, when it comes right down to it, the best way to slow down the increase in extreme weather events is to reduce the amount of carbon dioxide being released into our atmosphere.

OCEANS OF PLASTIC

Almost all the water on Earth is contained in the oceans. Oceans are so wide and so deep that humans dump all sorts of garbage into them, thinking it will disappear without causing any problems. We dump oil, fertilizers, pesticides, mountains of poop, and even radioactive waste into our oceans! But these days, it's plastic that worries scientists the most. In the Pacific Ocean, between Hawaii and California, an enormous collection of garbage has formed. It is called the Great Pacific **Garbage Patch**. Some scientists say it's twice the size of Texas and has 87,000 tons of plastic in it. It's mostly made up of **microplastics**. These are tiny pieces of plastic less than a quarter of an inch long (see p. 35). These microplastics are floating in the water like grains of pepper in a soup, and together they stretch from the surface down to the bottom of the sea. You could travel through the patch on a boat without even noticing it's there. This is the most famous garbage collection in the ocean, but it isn't the only one. There are four more: another in the Pacific, two in the Atlantic, and one in the Indian Ocean. If we don't do something about our waste, by 2050, there could be more pieces of plastic in the sea than fish!

BEFORE

The oceans hold 97 percent of the water on Earth and cover 70 percent of the planet's surface.

Around 250,000 species have been found in the oceans. Scientists think there are many more, probably millions, that have yet to be discovered (see p. 24). More than 80 percent of our oceans haven't been fully explored yet.

WHY STOP POLLUTING THE SEAS?

 Fish and other marine animals get tangled up in some types of trash, like fishing nets and plastic can holders. This can kill them.

 Sea creatures mistake microplastics (see p. 35) for food. After eating them, they feel full, so they stop eating real food. Many die. If we eat fish that have eaten microplastics, our health could suffer too.

 Lots of the trash in the sea ends up back on beaches. Trash spoils the beauty of the beach and is dangerous to the creatures that live on the beach.

 Oceans absorb nearly 30 percent of the carbon dioxide humans produce. But carbon dioxide makes the sea more acidic, which damages coral reefs. The more carbon dioxide the ocean absorbs, the more harmful it is (see p. 44).

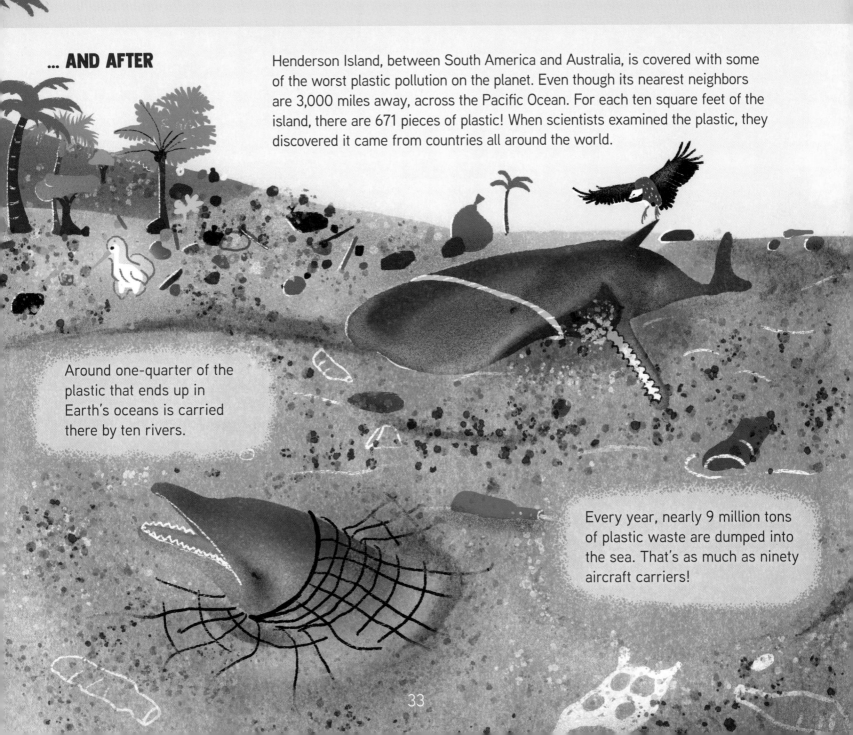

... AND AFTER

Henderson Island, between South America and Australia, is covered with some of the worst plastic pollution on the planet. Even though its nearest neighbors are 3,000 miles away, across the Pacific Ocean. For each ten square feet of the island, there are 671 pieces of plastic! When scientists examined the plastic, they discovered it came from countries all around the world.

Around one-quarter of the plastic that ends up in Earth's oceans is carried there by ten rivers.

Every year, nearly 9 million tons of plastic waste are dumped into the sea. That's as much as ninety aircraft carriers!

WHY DOES IT HAPPEN?

Most sea pollution comes from garbage. From fishing nets to single-use plastics like cigarette filters, bottles, straws, cups, balloons, bags, and corks. Nearly all this garbage (80 percent) comes from land. The other 20 percent is garbage released at sea, like discarded fishing gear. Pollution also comes from fertilizers, pesticides, and other chemicals. Even the gasoline that cars drip onto the road is washed away by rain and into the sea.

HOW DOES IT HAPPEN?

1. DIRECT SOURCES OF GARBAGE

Garbage can get into the sea directly when it is dumped on purpose or lost, like fishing nets or containers during storms.

2. INDIRECT SOURCES

Garbage can also get into the sea from indirect sources. Even cities hundreds of miles away from water wash garbage into storm drains when it rains. That garbage is carried by rivers to the sea. Tsunamis and cyclones can also move huge amounts of garbage into the sea.

HOW YOU CAN HELP

Cloth bag

Plastic bag

Once trash is in the sea, it is very difficult to get rid of it. So the best thing to do is to make sure it doesn't get there in the first place. In the European Union, plastic straws, silverware, plates, cups, and other **single-use** items are banned starting in 2021. You too could stop using disposable plastics and ask your friends and family to do the same. For example, use a bar of soap instead of liquid soap in plastic bottles. Or use refillable liquid soap. When it comes to single-use plastic, the best thing to do is avoid it all together.

3. BLOWING IN THE WIND

Wind can also carry garbage to the sea from far away, including from huge open-air dumps in places where there are no proper facilities for getting rid of garbage.

5. GARBAGE PATCHES

Some ocean currents turn like enormous whirlpools. They suck in trash and create gigantic patches of garbage in the sea. Currents also bring some of the trash back to land, where it ends up on beaches all over the world.

4. HOW MICROPLASTICS ARE FORMED

Once in the sea, a lot of plastic garbage is broken down into smaller and smaller pieces by sunlight and other physical forces. These tiny pieces are called microplastics.

HOW PEOPLE ARE HELPING

Removing plastic from the sea is difficult and expensive. But people are trying. When he was eighteen years old, Boyan Slat from the Netherlands created Ocean Cleanup. His group aims to remove 50 percent of the trash in the Great Pacific Garbage Patch. His system uses a floating U-shaped tube nearly 3,000 feet long. This traps the trash on the water's surface. A barrier that hangs down below stops it from escaping. But even if all the plastic in the sea is successfully removed, we can't keep making it and dumping it, or it will be an endless cycle. We need to stop plastic from getting into the sea in the first place!

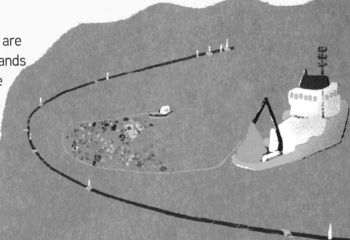

35

DESERTS AND DRY LAND

Did you know the Sahara, the biggest hot desert in the world, used to be green and dotted with lakes, rivers, and even forests? In that region, humid periods with a lot of rain alternate every 2,000 years with drier periods like now. But a study in 2017 found that humans may have made the current drought even worse. We introduced sheep, goats, and cows to the area, which ate all the plants. And we're still having an impact on nature today. The Aral Sea, for example, was once the fourth-biggest lake in the world. From 1960 on, it started getting smaller because the two rivers that flowed into it were diverted to water cotton fields. This caused one of the most serious environmental disasters humans have created. Today, the lake has almost disappeared.

BEFORE

Only 3 percent of Earth's water is fresh and drinkable. But 2.5 percent of that fresh water is not available because it is stored in glaciers, polar ice caps, and the atmosphere, or it's too far under Earth's surface to reach.

Dry regions, where rainfall is lowest, cover about 41 percent of our planet. More than 2 billion people live in these areas.

Nearly 44 percent of farmed land is in dry regions, but it produces around 60 percent of our food.

WHY STOP DESERTS FROM SPREADING?

We need soil to grow food. To feed the world's growing population, we'll probably need to produce 50 percent more food by 2050.

Most of Earth's fresh water is stored underground in soil and aquifers, layers of rock that water can move through. If those dry out, we'll lose most of our drinking water.

Drought leads to **desertification** (land becoming drier and the soil poorer). Drought kills more people than any other natural disaster. And it's very hard to predict when drought will happen and how long it will last.

More deserts means more sand lifted up by the wind. These sandstorms can give people serious breathing problems and pollute the water.

... AND AFTER

By 2025, 1.8 billion people will be living without enough water. This could lead to conflicts and even wars.

Every year, more than 46,000 square miles of land become sterile (unable to grow crops) because of desertification and drought. That's an area about the size of Pennsylvania.

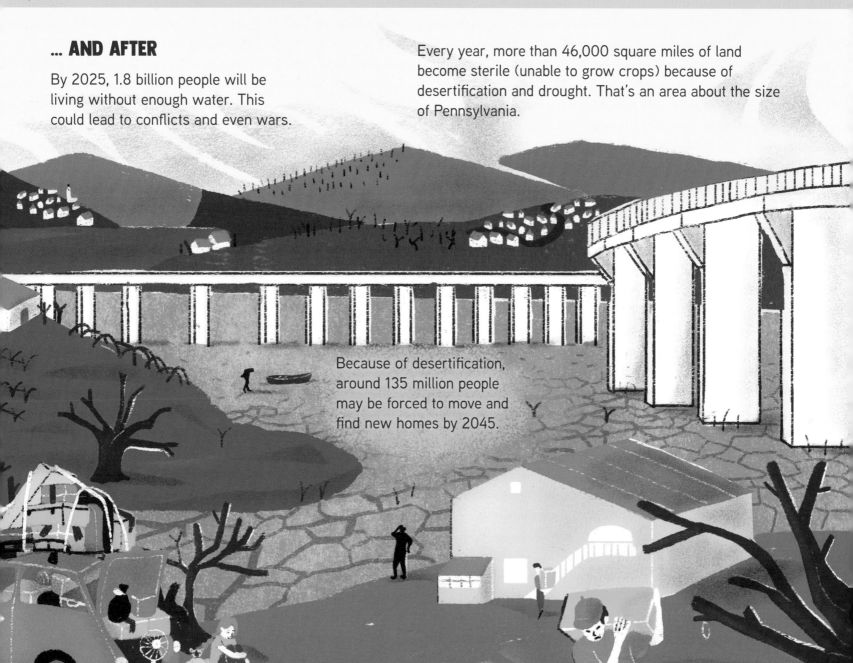

Because of desertification, around 135 million people may be forced to move and find new homes by 2045.

HOW DROUGHT WORKS

1. METEOROLOGICAL DROUGHT

Drought can be predicted in places where rainy and dry seasons alternate or where it hardly ever rains, like the Atacama Desert in South America. When a place has less rainfall than expected for a longer period of time, that is called meteorological drought.

2. HYDROLOGICAL DROUGHT

If it doesn't rain, especially when it's hot, water will eventually start disappearing from rivers, lakes, and underground pools. When these water reserves fall below average, it's called hydrological drought.

3. AGRICULTURAL DROUGHT

When there's not enough water in the soil for plants to grow, it's called agricultural drought. The land gets dry, and crops are lost.

HOW YOU CAN HELP

Even if you live in a place where there's plenty of water, don't waste it. Turn off the faucet while you brush your teeth. Wash fruits and vegetables in a tub of water. Make sure washing machines and dishwashers are fully loaded before you run them. Take a shower instead of a bath. A fifteen-minute shower uses ten to twenty gallons of water, while a bath uses sixty-six gallons! And green isn't always best for the environment. A front lawn is actually a pollutant because it needs to be watered a lot, takes energy to mow, and uses fertilizers to help it grow. If you have a green thumb, try **xeriscaping**. That's a way of gardening that uses as little water as possible.

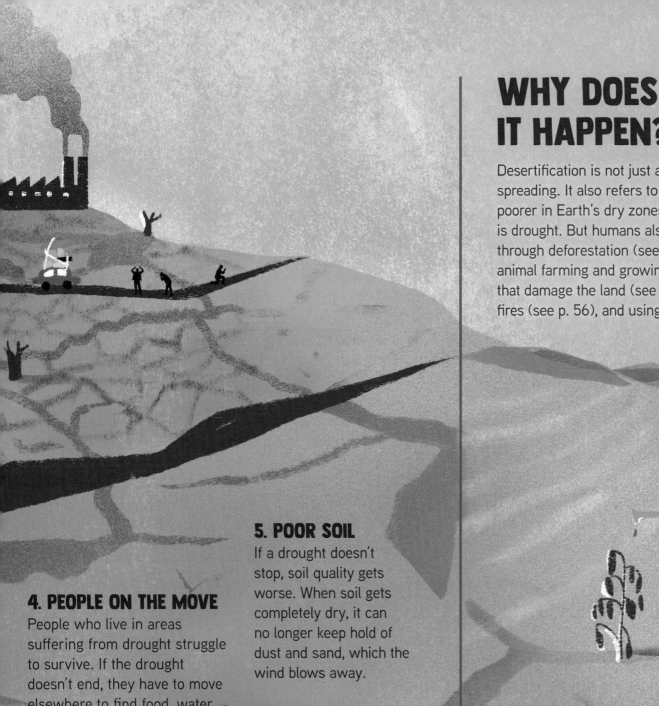

WHY DOES IT HAPPEN?

Desertification is not just about the desert spreading. It also refers to the soil becoming poorer in Earth's dry zones. The main cause is drought. But humans also play a part, through deforestation (see p. 12), intensive animal farming and growing crops in ways that damage the land (see p. 48), causing fires (see p. 56), and using too much water.

5. POOR SOIL

If a drought doesn't stop, soil quality gets worse. When soil gets completely dry, it can no longer keep hold of dust and sand, which the wind blows away.

4. PEOPLE ON THE MOVE

People who live in areas suffering from drought struggle to survive. If the drought doesn't end, they have to move elsewhere to find food, water, and fertile land to farm.

HOW PEOPLE ARE HELPING

In 2007, the Great Green Wall project started in Africa. The goal of the project is to plant millions of trees along the Sahel, a region south of the Sahara. The hope is to make 386,000 square miles of land fertile again. That's an area as big as Egypt! In China, the government began building a green wall nearly 3,000 miles long on the edge of the Gobi Desert to stop it spreading. Also in China, they've launched a project to create **sponge cities**. In these cities, roofs, roads, and other surfaces will be made from materials that can absorb, store, and reuse 70 percent of rainwater.

THE AIR THAT WE BREATHE

Did you know that clean air contains mostly nitrogen, rather than oxygen? But if the air is polluted, as it often is in big cities, we breathe in other gases that are bad for us: sulfur dioxide, nitrogen dioxide, carbon dioxide, and ozone, to name a few. And that's not all. Billions of microscopic particles hang in the air, like pollen, smoke, sand, and dust. These are called **particulate matter**. Together, gases and particles create **smog**. Smog is a mixture of smoke and fog that first became a problem in big cities when we started burning large quantities of coal in the early 1900s. In 1952, a blanket of smog covered London for five days and killed around 12,000 people! Today, coal burning is being limited or banned in many parts of the world. But the smog problem hasn't gone away. Most of Earth's population—91 percent—live in places where there are more pollutants in the air than is safe.

BEFORE When the air that we breathe is not polluted, it is made up of 78 percent nitrogen, 21 percent oxygen, and 1 percent argon and other gases (methane, hydrogen, carbon dioxide, and helium).

The nitrogen in our atmosphere was released in large quantities during the volcanic eruptions that took place when Earth was formed.

WHY PUT THE BRAKES ON AIR POLLUTION?

Smog is bad for our health. It leads to coughing, sneezing, itchy eyes, and headaches, which are no fun at all. It's a serious problem for our lungs, causing tumors and asthma. It's even more harmful to our heart, causing heart attacks and strokes.

Through a chemical reaction, sulfur dioxide in polluted air causes acid rain. Acid rain is harmful to animals and plants. It also damages buildings and monuments.

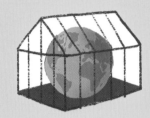

Smog is generally bad for the climate because it adds to the greenhouse effect (see p. 4).

... AND AFTER

Every year, 7 million people die earlier than they should because of air pollution.

Nine of the ten most polluted cities in the world are in India. In the US, Los Angeles and Bakersfield, California, usually have the worst air quality.

HOW SMOG WORKS

1. WINTER SMOG

When it's cold outside, car exhaust, factory smoke, and fumes from oil and coal heating systems create a haze in the sky. This haze contains various types of gas and particles, called primary pollutants. In some parts of the world, they call this winter smog.

2. PARTICULATES

Particles in the air, like pollen, grains of sand, smoke, and soot, come in many sizes. The smallest are even tinier than a hair's width. These are the most harmful, because they can get into the lungs and then the blood stream.

hair

particulate 2.5

particulate 10

HOW YOU CAN HELP

Walk, bike, or use public transportation whenever you can. If you have to use a car, use it wisely. For instance, why use two cars if everyone is traveling to the same place? Ask your parents to carpool with other families to save gas. Electricity also adds to smog, so turn out the light when you leave a room. If you're not using something, like a computer or a game console, turn it off. Better yet, unplug it. Even in standby mode, they still use energy. The digital messages we send also use energy. And with so many people sending messages that way, they have a huge impact on the environment. Don't send them just to pass the time. Become a tech ecologist!

3. SUMMER SMOG

When it's hotter and drier outside, sunlight reacts with nitrogen oxide and vapors produced by solvents, paints, and fuel. Some call this summer smog, a brownish-yellow haze that covers a city. It contains a variety of gases, including ozone. If ozone is high up in the atmosphere, it protects Earth from the sun's radiation. But ozone that is lower down in the air that we breathe can be harmful.

WHY DOES IT HAPPEN?

Transportation is one of the main causes of air pollution, especially when gasoline is used. There are more than a billion cars in the world and around 39,000 airplanes. Heating systems cause lots of pollution, especially in parts of the world where they still burn coal. Factories, garbage incinerators, and other systems that involve burning things also add to air pollution. The main natural causes of air pollution are volcanic eruptions, fires, and sandstorms.

HOW PEOPLE ARE HELPING

Many countries are switching to cleaner **renewable** sources of energy instead of fossil fuels like coal, oil, and gas that cause so much pollution. Wind turbines and hydroelectric power plants use the energy of wind and water to produce electricity. Solar panels "capture" the energy of the sun. The natural heat below Earth's surface, called geothermal energy, can also keep us warm. And when it comes to getting around, electric cars are becoming more and more popular. They do cause some pollution, but at least they don't poison the air. In China, a huge smog-free tower was built to make breathing easier. The tower sucks in polluted air, cleans it, and pumps it out again.

CORALS IN CRISIS

At first glance, corals look like very colorful rocks. But corals are actually animals. A single coral contains thousands of tiny creatures called polyps, which have very hard skeletons. Each polyp joins together with the skeletons of other polyps living in the same colony. Over thousands of years, they build up to form the coral reefs that are found in our tropical seas. Many people compare the reefs to rainforests, because although they occupy less than 1 percent of the surface of Earth, they are home to 25 percent of all ocean species. Coral reefs have 4,000 species of fish and 800 species of coral, as well as mollusks, sponges, and shellfish. The biggest is the Great Barrier Reef, off the coast of Australia. It is about 20,000 years old and covers 133,000 square miles. That's more than twice the size of Florida! Scientists consider it the biggest single structure made by living organisms on Earth, as well as one of the oldest.

BEFORE

Each year corals grow 0.3 inches to one inch in width and 0.3 to nine inches in height.

Corals grow in warm water, no more than 500 feet deep. That's because they need light from the sun to survive.

WHY SAVE CORAL REEFS?

Thousands of species of fish depend on the coral reefs to survive. Coral reefs' biodiversity is enormous and unique.

Many of the fish that we eat come from coral reefs. Reef fish provide food for at least 500 million people in the world.

Coral reefs protect the coast from waves, reducing waves' strength by 94 percent and their height by 84 percent.

... AND AFTER

Over the last thirty years, we have lost 50 percent of the world's coral reefs. Experts believe we are in danger of losing 90 percent by 2050.

From the first group of polyps, it takes 10,000 years for a coral reef to form.

HOW CORAL REEFS GET BLEACHED

1. HEALTHY CORALS

Corals and algae live in symbiosis. This means they depend on each other to survive. Tiny algae live inside the coral structures. And the algae are corals' main source of food and give them their color.

2. CORALS UNDER STRESS

When corals are stressed, they kick out the algae and gradually turn white. This bleaching is an alarm signal, like when we humans have a fever. The coral reefs can still recover, but if the stress continues, they can die.

HOW YOU CAN HELP

When you go to the beach, choose your sunscreen carefully. Studies show that some sunscreen ingredients, especially oxybenzone, can damage coral reefs. If you like to snorkel or scuba dive around coral reefs, don't touch or step on them. That kills corals. And never take corals from a reef or buy them as souvenirs.

3. DEATH OF THE CORAL

If the stress continues, the coral dies and seaweed grows over it, like a coat of fur.

WHY DOES IT HAPPEN?

There are lots of reasons why coral reefs get stressed. Mostly, it's because the ocean is getting warmer. Even a rise of just 1.8–3.6°F (1–2°C) is enough to bleach coral. Other causes of bleaching include too much sunlight when water levels are low, pollution dumped in the sea (see p. 33), and atmospheric pollution that makes the water more acidic. Some types of fishing are also extremely harmful. Cyanide fishing, for example, uses poison spray to stun and catch fish for aquariums. Some people fish using explosives or nets that damage coral reefs.

HOW PEOPLE ARE HELPING

In Florida, Erinn Muller and other researchers at the Mote Marine Laboratory have discovered a way to grow corals quickly and cheaply. Another researcher, Madeleine van Oppen, at the Australian Institute of Marine Science, is trying to breed algae and corals that are specially adapted to cope with higher temperatures. If these experiments are successful, researchers hope to transplant these "super corals" into existing coral reefs to make the reefs stronger.

FEEDING THE WORLD

Right now, there are 7.8 billion people on Earth. By 2050, that will go up to around 10 billion. To feed everyone, we will need a lot more farmland. Some say we'll need an area almost the size of Australia! This is a big reason why we've been farming animals and crops intensively for many years. We've been producing as much as possible using as little space as possible. Farmers use machinery and chemicals like fertilizers and pesticides. They keep animals shut inside huge sheds. But even with **intensive farming**, there are still millions of people who go hungry. We're still polluting the planet, and global warming is getting worse (see p. 4). We haven't solved the problem, and we're raising our food in an unsustainable way, using more resources than Earth can provide. That's partly because most of the crops we grow are to feed animals, rather than ourselves ... and then we eat the animals!

BEFORE   In 1900, we used around 9.6 million square miles for crops and animal grazing (about 20 percent of Earth's habitable land).

In 1961, around the world, each person ate an average of fifty-two pounds of meat a year.

WHY STOP INTENSIVE FARMING?

Intensive farming and animal farming are among the main reasons why humans are cutting down forests (see p. 12) and reducing biodiversity (see p. 24).

Fertilizers and animal poop pollute water (see p. 52), and pesticides can kill bees and other insects.

2,000

Producing meat uses far more resources than growing plants. For example, it takes more than 2,000 gallons of water to produce one pound of steak!

When ruminants (cows, sheep, and goats) fart and burp, they release a lot of methane (27 percent of all methane emissions). Methane is one of the greenhouse gases that cause global warming (see p. 4).

... AND AFTER These days, each person eats an average of ninety-seven pounds of meat each year. The countries that eat the most meat are the US, Kuwait, Australia, the Bahamas, and Luxembourg.

Today we use around 19 million square miles for grazing and crops (about 50 percent of Earth's habitable land).

There are nearly a billion cows and 23 billion chickens in the world.

HOW INTENSIVE FARMING WORKS

1. THE USE OF FERTILIZERS

If farmers use lots of fertilizers and don't rotate their crops, they can damage the soil and make it unusable. The layer of soil that is good for growing crops is only a couple of feet deep. It takes about 500 years to form just one inch of new soil.

2. FEEDING ANIMALS

During intensive farming, farmers keep animals inside sheds and don't let them outside to graze. Farmers give them food once a day, and the animals can eat and drink whenever they want. Sometimes, to fatten animals up more quickly, farmers add vitamins and hormones to the food.

3. SLURRY

When farmers clean all the animal poop and pee (called slurry) out of the sheds, they store it in huge pits. Like the animals' farts and burps, the slurry also produces greenhouse gases and risks polluting nearby water sources. Sometimes manure is used to fertilize fields or to make energy (called biogas), which is a better alternative for the planet.

HOW YOU CAN HELP

Vegetarians don't eat meat or fish. Vegans are vegetarian, but they also avoid foods produced by animals, like milk, eggs, and cheese. Some vegetarians and vegans eat this way to avoid killing animals or because they believe it is better for their health. Many scientists now say that reducing the amount of meat we eat will also help to fight climate change. You can help by eating less meat. Try eating it just one or two days each week. You can also choose to eat meat that isn't produced through intensive farming. Buy meat that is organic and free-range (check the labels on the package if you are unsure). Finally, avoid wasting meat. Don't put too much on your plate if you're not hungry and store leftovers for later.

WHY DOES IT HAPPEN?

Overpopulation is when there are too many people for the available resources. It is the main reason why we are intensively producing more food through agriculture, animal farming, and fishing. But what we choose to eat, and how much we eat, also plays a part. Humans are consuming more fish and meat than can be explained by the increasing population. Humans also waste lots of food. Roughly one-third of the food produced every year in the world for humans to eat—about 1.3 billion tons—gets wasted.

HOW PEOPLE ARE HELPING

Some farmers are switching to nonintensive and organic farming. These farmers use no pesticides and fewer natural resources. They farm the land, then let it rest for a while, so it stays fertile for longer. Some farmers are also trying **vertical farming**. They grow plants on roofs and inside buildings, using artificial light when necessary. To reduce the amount of methane produced by cows, scientists have discovered that you just need to add a special algae to their food. But some people believe the best way for us to fight global warming is for humans to eat less meat (or perhaps more insects)!

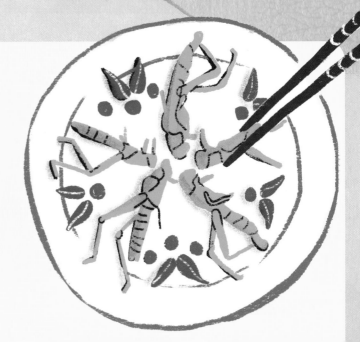

51

WHAT'S THAT IN THE WATER?

Eutrophication has a simple meaning: well-nourished. Sounds great, right? But, unfortunately, too much of a good thing can actually be bad—like eating too much candy. Similarly, it's bad for lakes and seas to take in too many nutrients. These nutrients include nitrogen, phosphorus, and ammonia, which is in fertilizers and detergents, as well as in pee and poop. For us, these are waste, but for algae and other plants, they are good food. Such good food that plants that eat them grow uncontrollably and produce a jelly-like substance called mucilage. Mucilage can spread in oceans and across beaches. Clear lakes are turned into green, smelly swamps. Fish and other aquatic animals die from lack of oxygen. Those waters become dead zones. Sadly, we're seeing more and more dead zones all around the world.

BEFORE

A 2014 study counted 117 million lakes on Earth. Lakes cover around 4 percent of Earth's land.

Eutrophication can happen naturally too, like when lakes get old and fill with sediment.

WHY STOP WATER EUTROPHICATION?

 When algae thrive, water gets murky and smelly.

 Plants, fish, and other animals living in algae-filled water are at risk of getting sick and dying.

 Eutrophication can also lead to **harmful algal blooms** (or HABs). This creates toxic or harmful effects in fish, shellfish, marine mammals, birds, and even humans.

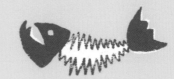 When plants and algae die, they release more carbon dioxide into the atmosphere, adding to global warming (see p. 4).

... AND AFTER

There are around 762 coastal areas affected by eutrophication. More than half of those are suffering from a lack of oxygen.

Eutrophication affects 54 percent of lakes in Asia, 53 percent in Europe, 48 percent in North America, 41 percent in South America, and 28 percent in Africa.

The Baltic Sea, in Northern Europe, contains seven of the ten biggest marine dead zones caused by eutrophication.

WHY DOES IT HAPPEN?

Nutrients that make algae grow too much come from four sources: crop farming, animal farming, sewage, and fossil fuels. The main cause of eutrophication, especially in the US and Europe, is crop farming. Fertilizers used for intensive farming have been increasing since 1960. Poop from farm animals and fish farming also feed the algae. Wastewater from homes and factories is another major source of eutrophication, especially in Asia, South America, and Africa. Finally, combustion from cars and other engines produces nitrogen oxide. This also adds to the problem.

HOW DOES IT WORK?

1. NUTRIENTS ARE ABSORBED

Nutrients, like the fertilizers used on fields, seep into the soil when it rains. From there, they are carried to the sea and lakes by rivers and underground aquifers.

HOW YOU CAN HELP

Phosphates are a nutrient for algae. Many countries have removed or limited phosphates in laundry soap and detergents. Check the labels on your cleaning products to make sure they are phosphate-free. Don't run the washing machine or dishwasher when it's half-full. If you used a pan to boil water, don't wash it at all. Did you know you can clean grease using a little vinegar instead of detergents?

2. A GREEN LAYER FORMS

The algae feed on the nutrients. They grow and reproduce quickly, forming a thick green layer on the surface of the water. This turns the water murky.

4. BACTERIA

Bacteria eat and digest the dead plants and algae. This releases more nutrients. At the same time, they absorb the remaining oxygen and release carbon dioxide.

5. FISH DIE

If they can't swim away, fish and other animals living in the water die because there's no more oxygen.

3. PLANTS DIE

The layer of algae stops sunlight from getting through (remember photosynthesis on p. 12). The plants underneath die because they get no light. Once they have eaten up all the nutrients, the algae die too.

HOW PEOPLE ARE HELPING

There are many ways to tackle eutrophication. We can clean wastewater, limit the use of fertilizers, find better ways of dealing with manure from farm animals, and regularly check the health of waterways above and below ground. Many countries are already doing these things. Another interesting idea is to breed lots of mussels and other mollusks. They filter water and help reduce any extra nutrients in it. Some countries around the Baltic Sea are doing this. Others are trying out nanobubbles. These are tiny bubbles of air that we can pump to the bottom of lakes. As the bubbles burst, they release oxygen and ozone. These help get rid of algae.

FIRE!

The fires raging across Australia and America in recent years have been shocking. The huge columns of smoke they create can be seen from outer space! Yet fire isn't always a bad thing. Fires can happen naturally. They are sometimes helpful to ecosystems. Fire can get rid of dangerous insects and plants that spread too fast. They clear out overgrown forests and make room for more light and rain to get through to plants. The ash that fires leave behind is great fertilizer. It helps flowers and fruit to grow. Fires are only a problem when they get too strong, go on for too long, and are difficult to control. That's the impact global warming is having on fires (see p. 4), in much the same way it's affecting cyclones (see p. 28).

BEFORE

Some plants need fire to survive. They grow again out of their own ashes. Lodgepole pine trees, for example, have seeds that are held in their cones by a drop of resin. The seeds only fall out when a fire's heat melts the resin.

Every year, nearly 1.3 million square miles of the planet's land burns. That's an area bigger than India.

WHY PREVENT EXTREME FIRES?

Big, uncontrolled fires destroy natural habitats and kill many animals that live there.

Fires are dangerous to humans—to our homes, our health, and even our lives. Breathing in smoke, especially over a long time, damages lungs and hearts.

Smoke from big fires can affect the climate in ways that scientists are still trying to understand. For example, smoke can reduce the amount of clouds and rain.

When trees burn, they release enormous amounts of carbon dioxide into the atmosphere. Once burned, they can no longer capture and store carbon dioxide (see p. 12).

... AND AFTER

In Australia, in the early 2020 fire season, more than 70,000 square miles of land were burnt. That's the size of North Dakota. The fires killed or displaced nearly 3 billion animals, including thousands of koala bears.

Fire season is the time of the year when fires are most common. Since 1980, because of climate change, fire season has gotten longer in at least 25 percent of areas that have forests, bush, or grasslands.

WHY DO THEY HAPPEN?

About 90 percent of fires are caused by humans. Campfires, cigarette butts, even sparks from a passing car are enough to start a fire. Lightning is the main natural cause, but sometimes volcanic eruptions can also start fires. Higher temperatures caused by climate change add to the problem.

HOW IT WORKS

1. THE FIRST SPARK

A fire needs three things to burn. This is called a fire triangle. Fire needs fuel (like a tree), a heat source to light the fuel (like a lightning bolt or a dropped match), and oxygen, which keeps the flames going.

HOW YOU CAN HELP

In a forest, never throw away anything that could start a fire, especially when the weather is hot and dry. Only light campfires in places where they're allowed, preferably in a fire pit or metal or stone ring. Always put campfires out entirely before you leave. Pour water over them and stir the coals to make sure all the embers are soaked. If you see a fire starting, call emergency services immediately.

2. THE FIRE SPREADS

When a fire finds new stuff to burn, it moves forward in a line, driven by the wind. The fire heats up the air in front of it, drying out wet surfaces, which then catch fire more easily.

3. FIRE TORNADOES

Gusts of wind can carry burning material far away from the original fire and start new fires. Sometimes, the fiercest fires can create their own powerful winds. These fiery tornadoes, traveling up to one hundred miles an hour, are very hard to predict.

4. PUTTING THE FIRE OUT

To stop a fire, firefighters sometimes burn wide areas ahead of a fire. This is called a firebreak. Then when the fire gets there, it has no fuel to burn. We can also douse fires with water or with fire retardant dropped from airplanes and helicopters. This stops the fire by reducing the heat and oxygen.

HOW PEOPLE ARE HELPING

We can fight fire with ... FUEGO! That's the name of a system for spotting fires invented by Carl Pennypacker, an American astrophysicist. He suggests we fit satellites, airplanes, towers, and drones with infrared sensors and video cameras that could spot fires faster. Then we could put them out before they grow too big. Eric Appel, a researcher at Stanford University, is developing a special gel to fight fires. His gel is harmless to the environment and can be sprayed on high-risk fire areas. The gel stops fires from starting.

TOO MUCH TRASH!

For years, we humans have been creating trash without much thought or care. We buy so many things, as though Earth's resources will last forever. We throw so many things away, as though our piles of trash will just disappear. Neither is true. Every year, we throw away around 330 million tons of plastic. That's the weight of 1.65 million blue whales, the biggest animals on the planet! And plastic is only 12 percent of the garbage we produce. There's also rubber and leather (2 percent), metals (4 percent), glass (5 percent), paper and cardboard (17 percent), and food (44 percent), as well as hazardous and radioactive waste. The problem is that our planet needs time to renew all the resources we take out of it. It needs time to absorb everything we throw away. Scientists have calculated that each year we use so much of what nature produces (our ecological footprint) that we actually need 1.7 planets like Earth to meet our demands. If we keep going like this, by 2050, we'll need two planets! While some scientists disagree with this calculation, everyone agrees that we must produce less trash.

BEFORE

Earth Overshoot Day is the day each year when we humans use up all the resources Earth can produce in twelve months. Back in 1971, we hit Earth Overshoot Day in December. That means we used up a year's worth of Earth's resources in a little less than one year. Not too bad.

WHY MAKE LESS TRASH?

Garbage produces gas that adds to the greenhouse effect (see p. 4), especially if it is burned or thrown into open-air dumps, which are still common in some parts of the world.

Garbage attracts rodents and insects that sometimes carry disease. When it's not disposed of properly, waste can pollute land and waterways.

Plastic is one of the main causes of sea pollution and puts many animal species in danger (see p. 32).

... AND AFTER

In 2019, we hit Earth Overshoot Day on July 29th. That means it took us just seven months to use up twelve months' worth of Earth's resources. Worldwide, we produce 2.2 billion tons of trash every year.

If we keep going like this, there will be 70 percent more trash by 2050. That's 3.75 billion tons each year!

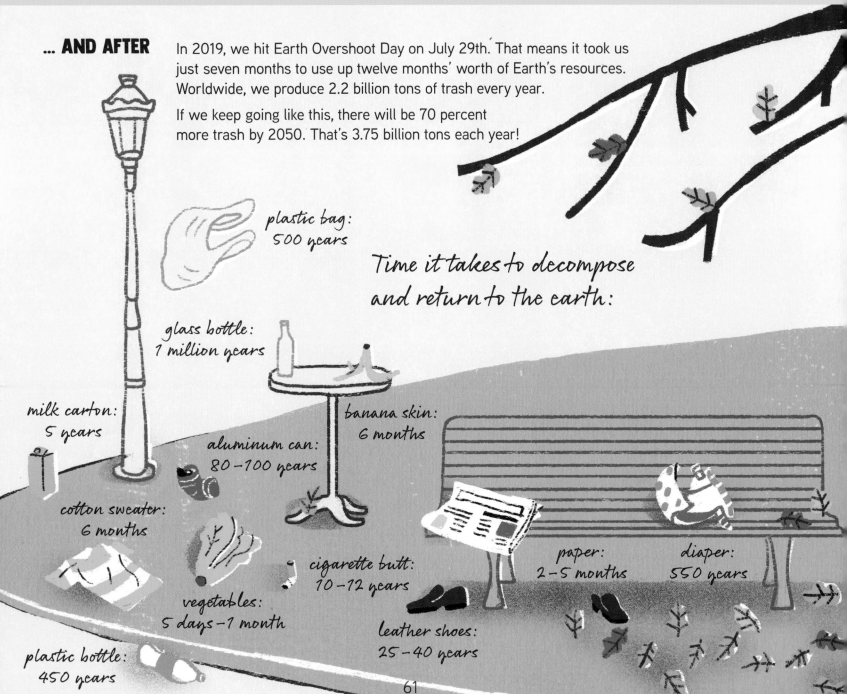

plastic bag:
500 years

Time it takes to decompose and return to the earth:

glass bottle:
1 million years

milk carton:
5 years

banana skin:
6 months

aluminum can:
80–100 years

cotton sweater:
6 months

cigarette butt:
10–12 years

paper:
2–5 months

diaper:
550 years

vegetables:
5 days–1 month

leather shoes:
25–40 years

plastic bottle:
450 years

61

HOW A PLASTIC BOTTLE IS RECYCLED

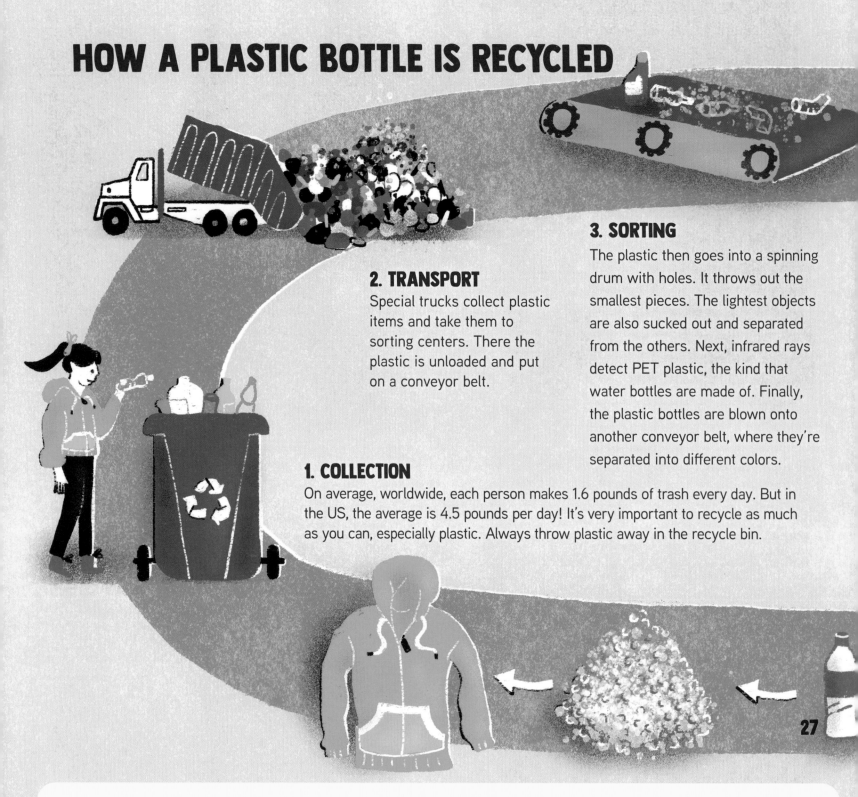

2. TRANSPORT
Special trucks collect plastic items and take them to sorting centers. There the plastic is unloaded and put on a conveyor belt.

3. SORTING
The plastic then goes into a spinning drum with holes. It throws out the smallest pieces. The lightest objects are also sucked out and separated from the others. Next, infrared rays detect PET plastic, the kind that water bottles are made of. Finally, the plastic bottles are blown onto another conveyor belt, where they're separated into different colors.

1. COLLECTION
On average, worldwide, each person makes 1.6 pounds of trash every day. But in the US, the average is 4.5 pounds per day! It's very important to recycle as much as you can, especially plastic. Always throw plastic away in the recycle bin.

27

HOW YOU CAN HELP

Have you heard the phrase "Reduce, Reuse, Recycle"? That's what we need to do with all our garbage. First, reduce how much plastic you use. A good way to reduce the amount of plastic you use is to buy loose, unpackaged foods from the bulk food section of your grocery store. They have all kinds of delicious stuff, from granola to dried mango. When you buy in bulk, you reduce the amount of plastic packaging you bring home. Second, reuse whatever you can. Instead of throwing away clothes or toys you don't want anymore, organize a garage sale with your friends. They are fun, and you can make some money too. If you have an electronic device that doesn't work anymore, get it repaired instead of throwing it out. Third, if you cannot reuse the item, recycle it. You can recycle almost anything, from batteries to bottles to books. Before you throw something away, look into if it can be recycled.

4. THE FIRST WASH

When plastic bottles get to the recycling plant, they go into a drum where they are washed with hot water and steam to get rid of the labels. Then a detector picks out things that shouldn't be there, like metal or the wrong kinds of plastic, which are removed.

5. CHOPPING UP AND THE SECOND WASH

A turning blade cuts up the bottles into small pieces. Then they're washed again, spun to get rid of extra water, and dried in a dryer. Finally, they are shredded into pieces about the size of cornflakes. Any dust is vacuumed away.

6. RECYCLING

Businesses buy these plastic flakes to use as raw material to make new things. For example, it takes flakes from twenty-seven plastic bottles to make a fleece coat.

HOW PEOPLE ARE HELPING

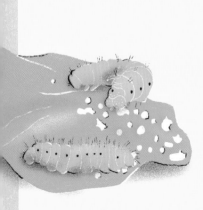

Several years ago, Italian researcher Federica Bertocchini discovered almost by chance that the wax moth caterpillar is able to eat and digest polyethylene. That is one of the most difficult types of plastic to dispose of. Scientists are now working to produce the caterpillars' digestive substance in a laboratory. This discovery could help solve the problem of disposing of polyethylene, which is so damaging to the environment. Likewise, an international team of scientists, led by Professor John McGeehan, from the UK, has created an enzyme that breaks down plastic bottles. The breakthrough happened after the discovery of plastic-eating bugs at a Japanese dump. It could help solve the global plastic pollution crisis by fully recycling bottles.

Also, Precious Plastic is a nonprofit group in the Netherlands that is teaching people how to make their own plastic recycling machines. With these simple machines they build at home, people are recycling plastic into all kinds of cool things. Everything from chairs and tables to jewelry and watches! Get all the blueprints you need at preciousplastic.com.

SPREAD THE WORD!

Climate change is a huge problem for Earth and all of its inhabitants. If we don't take action right now and change how we live on this planet, many plant and animal species will go extinct, and life for humans will become very difficult.

Everything on planet Earth is connected. Humans, animals, plants, the ocean, the atmosphere—we are all linked, and if one thing is unhealthy, the rest will suffer. We humans have the ability to change our actions and change our planet. Some people are doing just that. Around the world, many people, groups, and even whole governments are working on the problem of climate change. Humans are coming up with many different solutions that could reduce the negative impacts and hopefully turn things around.

There is no end to the actions you can take every day to help our planet recover from climate change. You can follow the suggestions in this book and come up with many more ideas of your own!

But the most powerful thing you can do is speak up and get your friends and family to join you.

In fact, young people just like you are already leading the fight. Environmental activist Greta Thunberg was just fifteen years old when she began protesting outside parliament in Sweden, where she lived. She demanded that her government take stronger action to combat climate change. Soon other students learned of her actions and began organizing their own protests and strikes, first in Sweden and then all around the world. Greta's protests turned into a global movement. She inspired millions of people around the world. They began demanding change in their own countries.

Greta didn't start out thinking she would become a world leader. She started reducing her own consumption, recycling more, and asking her family to join her efforts. You can do the same.

Your small actions add up and make a difference.

Spread the word to everyone you know. When you get others involved, like Greta did, the change is even bigger. The movement to stop climate change happens one person at a time.

Today that person is *you!*

YOU CAN BE A PART OF THE SOLUTION!

LEARN MORE ABOUT ORGANIZATIONS WORKING COLLECTIVELY TO PROTECT OUR FUTURE.

Friends of the Earth

foei.org

Greenpeace

greenpeace.org

Ocean Conservancy

oceanconservancy.org

One Tree Planted

onetreeplanted.org

Sierra Club

sierraclub.org

World Wildlife Fund (WFF)

worldwildlife.org

MAKE A DIFFERENCE AND HELP CHANGE THE WORLD WITH CITIZEN SCIENCE.

ANIMALS
Celebrate Urban Birds

celebrateurbanbirds.org

Lost Ladybug Project

lostladybug.org

Project Feederwatch

feederwatch.org

Project Squirrel

projectsquirrel.org

BIODIVERSITY
inaturalist

inaturalist.org

TREES AND PLANTS
BudBurst

budburst.org

TreeSnap

treesnap.org

WATER
Blue Water Task Force

surfrider.org/programs/
blue-water-task-force

Earth Eco Water Challenge

monitorwater.org

WEATHER
**Community Collaborative Rain,
Hail & Snow Network**

cocorahs.org

NASA GLOBE Observer

observer.globe.gov

GLOSSARY

Anthropocene: What some people call the time we live in. It means that humans are having a major impact on the natural environment.

atmosphere: The gases surrounding Earth.

biodiversity: The variety and quantity of animals, plants, and all things living in a place.

carbon dioxide (CO$_2$): A heavy, colorless gas that is part of breathing and decaying processes.

citizen scientist: People who aren't professional, trained scientists but who help collect data used by scientists.

climate change: Increasing changes in many environmental patterns over a long time.

cryosphere: The part of Earth that is covered in snow and ice.

deforestation: The cutting down of lots of trees or whole forests in order to use the land for something else.

desertification: Land becoming drier and soil becoming poorer.

emissions: The gases we produce and release.

eutrophication: Too many nutrients in water, which causes too many plants to grow. This creates a lack of oxygen, which can kill animals living in the water.

extinction: An entire species being wiped out and no longer existing anywhere. Mass extinction is a huge drop in several species over a short period of time.

fossil fuel: A fuel (such as coal and natural gas) formed long ago from dead organisms. This fuel is limited because more cannot be made.

garbage patch: A big cluster of garbage that wasn't intentionally made and isn't where garbage should be. The Great Pacific Garbage Patch is a floating island of garbage that was formed when currents in the Pacific Ocean pushed pieces of trash together.

global warming: The process of Earth getting hotter overall and over time.

green roof: A roof deliberately planted with trees and other plants.

greenhouse effect: Earth's atmosphere trapping some of Earth's heat, like glass holds heat inside a greenhouse.

greenhouse gas: The gases in Earth's air that trap the sun's heat. The most common greenhouse gases are water vapor, carbon dioxide, and methane.

guerrilla gardener: A person who plants flowers and other plants in empty public lots.

harmful algae bloom (HAB): When algae consume too many nutrients, they grow too big and pollute the water, harming animals in the water.

heat island: A place that gets extra hot. A city is an example.

heat wave: When it is hotter than usual for five days or more.

intensive farming: Producing as much as possible in as little space as possible. This requires harmful and unsustainable practices, such as using machinery too often on land, using toxic chemicals, and penning animals in tight spaces.

living shoreline: A deliberately created marsh, forest, or wall made of plants that creates a barrier between the sea and a city.

microplastics: Tiny pieces of plastic less than a quarter of an inch long.

natural habitat: The place where a plant or animal can most easily survive.

overpopulation: Too many people or other animals for the resources that are available.

ozone: The layer of Earth's atmosphere that filters the sun's ultraviolet rays.

particulate matter: Microscopic particles, such as pollen, smoke, sand, and dust, that are in polluted air.

permafrost: Areas of Earth that are always frozen.

photosynthesis: How plants make their own food. This process uses sunlight, carbon dioxide, and water and releases oxygen back into the air.

polar ice caps: Enormous masses of ice covering huge portions of the Antarctic and Greeland.

pollution: The introduction of toxic substances to our environment.

reforestation: The act of regrowing a forest by planting seeds or young trees.

renewable energy: Energy made from resources, such as wind, water, and sun, that nature can replace.

single-use plastics: Plastics that can be used only one time and are then thrown away.

smog: A mixture of smoke and fog.

sponge city: A city where the roofs, roads, and other surfaces are made from materials that absorb, store, and reuse 70 percent of rainwater.

transpiration: When plants absorb water through their roots and then release it through tiny holes under their leaves.

vertical farming: Growing crops on roofs or inside buildings instead of spread out in fields.

xeriscaping: Gardening with as little water as possible.

INDEX

Blue Dot Kids Press

www.BlueDotKidsPress.com

Original English-language edition published in 2021 by Blue Dot Kids Press, PO Box 2344, San Francisco, CA 94126. Blue Dot Kids Press is a trademark of Blue Dot Publications LLC.

Original English-language edition © 2021 Blue Dot Publications LLC

Original English-language edition translated by Emma Mandley and edited by Michelle McCann

Italian-language edition © 2020 Dalcò Edizioni Srl, Via Mazzini n. 6, 43121 Parma, Italy. All rights reserved. rights@dalcoedizioni.it. www.dalcoedizioni.it.

BLUE D●T KIDS PRESS

To request permissions or to order copies of this publication, contact the publisher at www.BlueDotKidsPress.com.

Cataloging in Publication Data is available from the United States Library of Congress.

ISBN: 9781735000534

Paper in this book is certified against the Forest Stewardship Council™ standards. FSC™ promotes environmentally responsible, socially beneficial, and economically viable management of the world's forests.

Printed in China with soy inks.

First Printing

SOURCES

Air Quality Life Index, aqli.epic.uchicago.edu

Alleanza Italiana per lo Sviluppo Sostenibile, asvis.it

Consorzio nazionale per la raccolta, il riciclo e il recupero degli imballaggi in plastica, corepla.it

Center for Climate and Energy Solutions, c2es.org

Ecological Footprint Calculator, footprintcalculator.org

Earth Overshoot Day, overshootday.org

Food and Agriculture Organization of the United Nations, fao.org

Fridays For Future, fridaysforfuture.org

Global Forest Watch, globalforestwatch.org

Intergovernmental Panel on Climate Change, ipcc.ch

IUCN Red List, iucnredlist.org

MIT Technology Review, technologyreview.com

Mongabay, rainforests.mongabay.com

NASA Climate Kids, climatekids.nasa.gov

NASA Earth Observatory, earthobservatory.nasa.gov

NASA Global Climate Change, climate.nasa.gov

National Ocean Service, oceanservice.noaa.gov

Nature, nature.com

New Scientist, newscientist.com

NOAA SciJinks, scijinks.gov

Science Learning Hub, sciencelearn.org.nz

Scientific American, scientificamerican.com

Smithsonian Magazine, smithsonianmag.com

Submariner Network, submariner-network.eu

United Nations Convention to Combat Desertification, unccd.int

United Nations Environment Programme, unenvironment.org

UN Sustainable Development Goals, un.org/sustainabledevelopment

US Bureau of Reclamation, usbr.gov

Weather Wiz Kids, weatherwizkids.com

World Bank Group, worldbank.org

World Health Organization, who.int

WWF, worldwildlife.org